Brody's Fur-Ever Home

A story of love and loss

Lori J. Cooper

Archway Publishing books may be ordered through booksellers or by contacting:

Archway Publishing
1663 Liberty Drive
Bloomington, IN 47403
www.archwaypublishing.com
1 (888) 242-5904

Because of the dynamic nature of the Internet, any web addresses or links contained in this book may have changed since publication and may no longer be valid. The views expressed in this work are solely those of the author and do not necessarily reflect the views of the publisher, and the publisher hereby disclaims any responsibility for them.

Interior Image Credit: Stacy Hummel

ISBN: 978-1-4808-8107-5 (sc)
ISBN: 978-1-4808-8108-2 (e)

Print information available on the last page.

Archway Publishing rev. date: 08/13/2019

Brody's Fur-Ever Home: A story of love and loss

By Lori J. Cooper

I was born around April 22nd, 2018 on a farm in Arizona. My cat mother did the best she could to help me, my sister, and my brother to adjust to our new life. I had fun playing with all of the animals on the farm, and when my human Mom took me into her home to foster me for adoption, I was excited to have so many cat brothers and sisters to play with!

One day in August, something happened to my eye. My foster Mom noticed my right eye was red and hurting. She took me to a Veterinary doctor to get medicine for my eye. In order to find my fur-ever home, my foster Mom took me to an adoption center where human Moms and children would hold me and look at me to see if they wanted to adopt me and take me home. Because my eye looked different, no one wanted to adopt me. I went to the adoption center with my foster Mom a few times, but I always came back to my foster home. I was sad and did not know if I would ever be adopted. Everyone was afraid of me and thought I was ugly.

Then, one day in October, I went to the adoption center again. When I got there, I hid under a table. A nice woman called out to me to come see her, and she was telling me I was "beautiful". She held me, and kissed me, and I looked up into her eyes and reached up to touch her face. When I did this, she called me a "love bug". I felt a spark inside! I got excited, and started to purr. I knew that she was going to be my Mom! I was so excited to go home with her and meet my new brother Grayson and sister Alli. My Mom said I was "going to love it!" I finally had a fur-ever home!

I met my cat brother Grayson, and sister Alli. They sniffed me and I sniffed them, and I knew this was going to be a great home for me! I think we were a bit scared of each other, but we got along just fine. They were curious about my eye looking different, but it didn't seem to bother them. They accepted me just the way I was!

For the first few weeks while I was settling in, I followed my Mom around the house. Everywhere she went, I would go too! When she worked on her computer, I would lay on her lap. My mom would sometimes have to go to work. When my Mom came home, she would yell for me, saying "Where is my baby Brody?", "Where is my love-bug?" I would immediately go to the door to greet her and get a treat and lots of kisses and cuddles.

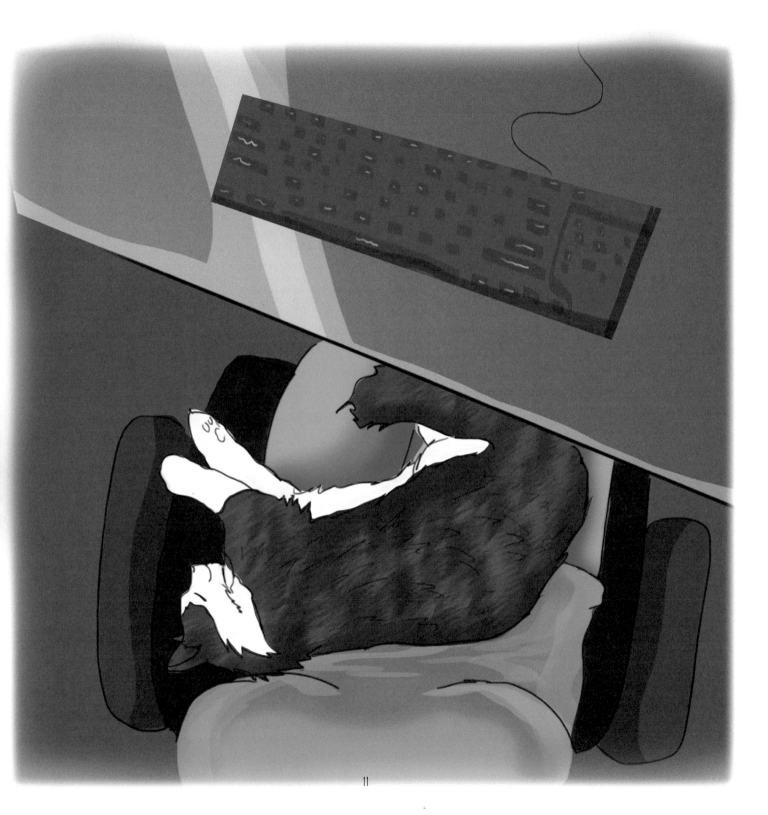

At the end of November, my Mom told my Dad she thought I was getting too thin, and that something was wrong, because my belly got big. She said I had a "potbelly", and she could feel my bones and thought I was too skinny. My Mom knew something was wrong, so she called the Veterinary doctor. The day before the doctor came to my house to see me, I was so tired I did not want to get out of bed.

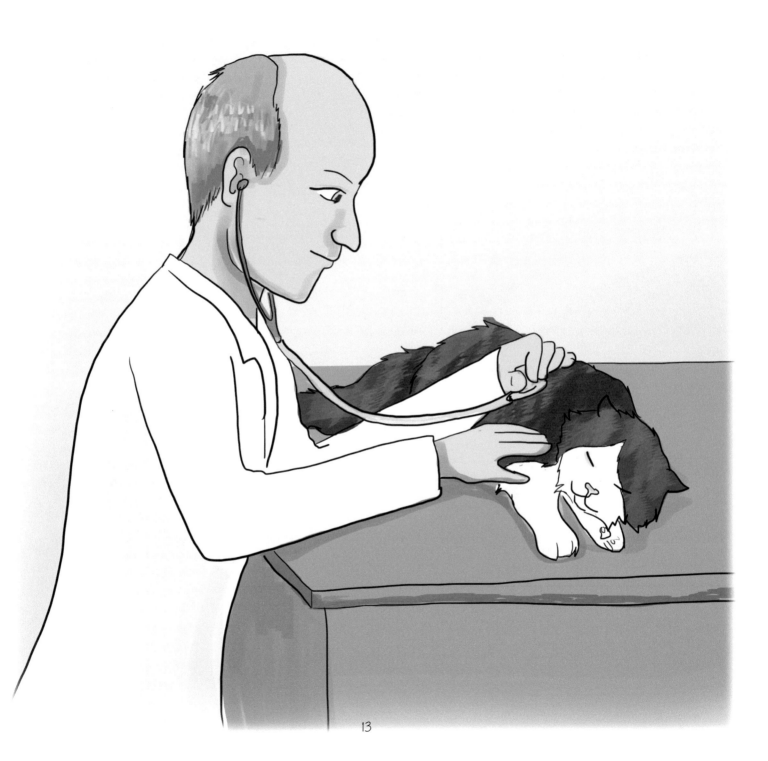

My Mom would put me on the counter to drink because I had trouble jumping and I would sit and stare up and her to be held. I would sit by my water dish and drink. I felt hot and sick. I threw up, and Mom called the doctor to come right away. The Veterinary doctor came and took me for testing. When the Doctor brought me home, he had bad news.

The doctor told my Mom that I was sick and would not get better. He explained to her that my "potbelly" was fluid in my tummy and I was infected with something called Feline Infectious Peritonitis" or F.I.P. I did not know what F.I.P. was, but it sounded scary and made my Mom cry. When Mom told my family, she started to cry and told them we did not have much time left to spend together.

My Mom was desperate to find help. She contacted Veterinary Doctors and researchers all over the United States, but she did not receive good news. All of the doctors' agreed, I was running out of time, and I would not live much longer. Soon after, my Mom got a call from the Veterinary Doctor who had more bad news. I also had Feline Leukemia. The Leukemia was in my blood. My Mom was so upset that she could not stop crying.

Two days later, I could not greet my Mom at the door like I usually would. I was so tired; I could not get out of my cubby in my cat tree. My Mom carried me out to the couch, where I liked to sit on my blanket and she could cuddle with me. She let me sit in the sun, drink some water, and lay with her while she sang to me and pet me. Mom prayed to God that I would have a happy life in Heaven and not have any more pain. She told me she was sorry for my short time on earth and thanked God for letting me have 6 weeks with her, where I could be loved and "live like a King" my Dad would say.

The veterinary Doctor said he would be coming to our house in the evening, so my Mom spent all day with me cuddling, loving and telling me she would love me forever. My Mom called my Dad to come home from work and told my human brother Ethan when he got home from school that it was time to say goodbye to me and I was going home to Heaven. My Mom made sure that in my short little life that my fur-ever home was the best, most loving place a baby kitty like me could have!

The Veterinary doctor showed up to my house a little after 5:00 p.m. He told my Mom that she was a good Mom and that there was nothing more anyone could do for me. He told her he could tell that I was loved very much and this was not her fault. He said that I was "lucky to have such a wonderful adopted family to love me for 6 weeks". I laid down on my Mom's lap, and the doctor gave me a shot, so I could go to sleep.

Sometime after 6:00 p.m. on December 14th, 2018, I went to sleep in my Mom's arms. I could hear her tell me how much she loved me. She told me "how special" I was, and how I made her "so happy." My Mom promised me that she would love me forever and while she was so sorry I had to leave her and my new family, she was not sorry for our love, or for the fun time we got to spend together. She told me God would love me and take care of me, and she would "see me again someday". My Mom told me that God works in mysterious ways and He must have needed me home with Him for a bigger reason. Mom told me, I get to be "an Angel!" Although I will miss my Mom, I get to be with her and my family every day in their hearts and memories. God made me special and I was able to have a loving home, even though I looked different. Everyone deserves to be loved. I had the best fur-ever home and I was so lucky to be loved!

In the summer, my Mom got a message from the shelter where she adopted me that they had a special baby kitty for her. They told her the new baby reminded them of me. My Mom was hesitant to visit the shelter because she felt it was too soon and she did not want to feel like she was replacing me. Later that week, my Mom met my brother "Bear" and he reached out to her and cuddled with her the way I used to. My Mom prayed about adopting Bear, and asked God to guide her in this decision. She brought my brother Bear home a couple of weeks later. My Mom tells people "God sent Bear" to her, to heal her heart from losing me. Mom believes that I picked Bear out for her, so she would not miss me so much. Bear has the best home a kitty could have!

"Someday, we will all be reunited again, but until that day comes, Bear will heal my Mom's heart and be loved by her just like I was."

The End

Printed in the United States
By Bookmasters